THE
CENTER

HOW OUR THOUGHTS, FEELINGS, AND BELIEFS SHAPE OUR DESTINY

Nicole,
Queen you are amazing.
Continue to grow and
always believe in god.

ANTONIO JAVAR HAIRSTON

ISBN: 978-0-578-41477-5
Library of Congress Control Number: 2018914126

Editing by: Valentina Alexandre
Front cover image by: Duane Bonaparte

Antonio Javar Hairston
Antonio Javar Hairston Publishing
New York, New York

Printed and bound in the United States of America
First 2019
AntonioJavar.com

DEDICATED TO:

My beautiful mother, Pinkie Gibson-Key, my grand-mother, Jeannette Wright, my aunts, Betty Wright and Ruby Key-Wright. Your wise guidance, support, and unconditional love has brought me back to my center over and over again.

And to whomever is reading this book, I hope it brings you peace, clarity, and most of all, your best centered life.

CONTENTS

PREFACE

The year was 2012. I'd just graduated from college, and I was lost as hell on what to do next. I'd graduated with all these honors including being the top public relations graduate of the year at my university, and yet here I was, feeling lost and confused about the next step. The only reason I studied PR was because it was the only thing even remotely close to something I wanted to do. I've always been into entertainment and I consider myself a people's person too. Working in PR just seemed like the next logical step to doing something that felt like who I am. Now don't get me wrong, I liked PR, but I absolutely did not love it. I cared for it, but it wasn't sending chills through my body and igniting passion in me so intensely that I was jumping out of bed in the morning screaming, God, I love what I do! Therefore, I knew there had to be something else or something more.

When I moved to New York in 2013, almost ten

months after graduation, I knew my life was truly beginning, and I was going to pursue my biggest dreams and desires. I didn't know all the specifics; I just knew that my story, my life, was about to change forever. And it did.

Rewind a little bit to when I moved back home to Miami literally the day after graduation; I began my journey of asking myself questions like, What is it that you really love to do, Antonio? What could you see yourself doing for eternity even if you weren't getting paid? I began to really do some research within myself about life and where I wanted to be and where I wanted to end up. Oftentimes, I felt my questions just led me to more questions. I couldn't seem to get to the deepest level of clarity that I was yearning for. I always had this feeling that there was something massive and important for me to do in this world. I simply just wanted to feel that I was moving in that direction. Of course, to others it was like, oh wow! you just graduated; we are so proud of you, blah blah blah. I wasn't necessarily feeling the same sentiments. Has that ever happened to you? Other people saying they are proud of you, but you have this feeling and knowing that you can do more? It was one of those things.

I will never forget I was sitting at my grandmother's kitchen table during one of those uncertain times doing some job searching and YouTube browsing, when I came across this video by the great Dr. Norman Vincent Peale on the power of positive thinking. From that video, YouTube began suggesting to me a plethora of other videos from prolific teachers like Jim Rohn to Napoleon Hill to Catherine Ponder. It was exactly what I needed at the time and in that moment. I'd heard about the power of positive thinking before, but after that day, I began studying it intensively along with meditation, emotions and hundreds of self-help books, ideas, thoughts, and teachings.

This book is really about the summary of what years of experience, studying, and knowledge has done and is doing for me in my life and what I believe it could do for you in yours as well.

Fast forward to 2016, when I finally was able to visit a place I've dreamed about visiting for years; Rio De Janeiro, Brazil. I fell in love with Brazil after watching a concert there from my favorite singer, Whitney Houston. I remember watching her perform there and thinking, Wow, the energy of the people there was something I'd never seen before. They matched her vibrant energy on stage to the tee. The audience knew every single word, they knew every adlib, and they were in the moment. It was something that made me think, I've got to go to Brazil.

The experience was everything I imagined and more. From the first day, the energy of the people, their smiles, their joy, was intoxicating.

I made sure I didn't spend all my time there lying on the beach sipping Pina Coladas either. I visited the inner cities and small towns. I danced with the locals all night to the beat of soca. I visited villages and communities infused with bright, organic, lively and harmonious art. I meditated on Brazil's finest beaches in Ipanema and Copacabana. And yes, I partied too.

This trip was aligning me with my center in every way. I felt clear-minded, peaceful, and like something astonishing was going to happen to me when I returned home. I was right.

You see, right before leaving Rio De Janeiro, Brazil, a friend of mine took this picture of me meditating with the beautiful greenish bluish ocean behind me and these glorious mountains behind the ocean and the sun shining bright, it was a magical moment, and you can feel it when you look at the picture. A few weeks later when I

returned from Brazil, I was looking at that picture intensely, reminiscing on what that moment felt like, trying to capture it again in my mind and BOOM! That's when the title of this book popped into my head; THE CENTER! I knew right then and there what I wanted to write about and why.

What is the center? The center is the seat of your soul. It's where your greatest potential to live an incredible life by design resides. You know your center really well because it is where you feel the most joy. The CENTER is within you. The center is within me. The center is within everyone. Now, your ability to feel your center, to understand it, and to live your life predominantly from it, is a totally different story. This book is about how our thoughts, feelings, and beliefs can hinder you from feeling and living in your center. On the other hand, this book is also about how our thoughts, feelings and beliefs can yield to us the power to align with our center and witness the power of miracles in our lives.

Too often, we think that the answers to our problems in life are outside of us. We spend our lives trying to keep up with the Joneses or get what the next person has when truly everything we need is inside of us. Realizing and accepting that is usually where we find ourselves often struggling.

Do you ever feel like you simply don't know the next step to take in life? Perhaps you feel like you know the next step to take but don't know how to go about taking that next step.

When you're not aligned with your center, you feel lost, confused and out of touch with the vision for your life. You feel like everyone in the world is just doing their own thing and you are too. You live life from a very limited and small point of view. When you don't live life from the center, you live consciously unconscious.

You worry about problems that if you were centered, you wouldn't. In your center, inspiration finds you like a light finds darkness in a room and transforms it right before your eyes.

What you are about to read is incalculably powerful.

It has the potential to literally set your life onto a new trajectory and change it forever. This book is a tool for your mind, soul, and spirit. It will allow you to dive deep into the inner recesses of your mind, heart and consciousness. I would say before you read this book, clear your mind of what you think it might be about. Leave your mind open to learning something new or perhaps hearing something you already know in a different way. If you apply even half of what's in this book, you'll become greater and experience a powerful surge in clarity in every area of your life. The center. It's the place where inspiration, love, and ultimately, your success in life comes from. Without it, nothing is possible.

CHAPTER 1

You've Been Conditioned without Your Permission

The Setup

What you are about to read is powerful and real. It has the potential to literally set your life onto a new trajectory and change it forever. This book is a tool for your mind, soul, and spirit. If you truly open your heart as you are reading, it will allow you to dive deep into the inner recesses of your thoughts, heart, and inner consciousness. First however, you must give yourself permission to do that. Open yourself up to receive knowledge that you may not know that you don't know, that you don't know. When you approach this book from that perspective, it will allow you to gain and understand things you probably wouldn't have if you didn't approach it from that perspective.

If you use this book actively and intentionally,

you'll become a greater version of yourself and you will experience a powerful surge of clarity in every area of your life; beginning at the center of your very being. The center isn't a physical space but it's more like the seat of your soul. It's the place where inspiration, love, and ultimately your success in life comes from. Without it, nothing is possible.

Understand this, your environment has already had the chance to cultivate who you are before you did. Your name, birthplace, family, living arrangements, and pretty much your whole identity were picked out for you.

No matter where, when, or to whom you were given an identity. You were conditioned without your permission. And of course, how could you have not been? We were all infants at one time; helpless, fluffy bundles of joy with no knowledge of the world, and in need of guidance and love from our caretakers. This identity has been the foundation for your life. This identity most likely has completely formed who you are today. It's given you wonderful things and perchance not so wonderful things, allowing you to view the world in a specific way. Perhaps your parents were Buddhist, or Christian, and you therefore grew up embracing those religions or maybe rejecting them.

Maybe you grew up in a military family, and that made you value traveling around the world or staying put in one place. Or maybe your parents were racist and this made you want to stand up for the rights of others. Maybe you grew up being picked on because of the way you looked or how you acted, and if so, those experiences have had a powerful and detrimental impact on who you have become today.

Take two to three minutes to think about some conditions that you grew up under that may be impacting who you are today. Thought about it? Ready? Let's go!

So, I shared that to acknowledge that all of those factors are not necessarily a bad or a good thing, but they are a thing. Pre-conditioning is something that many people are not consciously aware of and therefore aren't able to correlate many of their thoughts, feelings, habits, and reasoning today to how they were conditioned as infants.

It's Good To Know

Why is knowing about the conditions and programs placed upon your life important? The real question is why isn't it? Recognizing and understanding the conditions that have dictated your life since birth is a major step to examining whether you want to begin changing those conditions or to continue to reinforce them, giving them more power in your life.

The Effects Of My Conditioning

My parents never married and were only together for five years. Growing up, I experienced violence, chaos and a lot of emotional pain. It wasn't all bad though. I also experienced love, bliss, and fun times with my family. All of it helped to create mindsets within me.

Growing up, my mother was a strong woman with an entrepreneurship spirit. At only five foot three, she could stand tall with the best of them. She was the kind of mother that didn't say I love you every single day, but felt that by making sure my brothers and I had clothes on our backs and food on the table, that she was showing love in her own special way. She was right. She dropped out of high school in the ninth grade and never looked back. Later in life she went to cosmetology school and opened up a successful beauty salon that she managed for twenty years and also became a nurse. She was twenty-seven when I was born.

My father on the other hand was nineteen when I was born and really wasn't ready for the responsibility of raising a child. This caused him to be absent most of the time. In his heart I knew he loved me, but he hadn't cultivated the right tools and knowledge it took to be a consistent, and strong presence in my life. A talented musician by nature, I gained many of my musical and speaking abilities from him. We weren't rich but we weren't poor either. Mom always made sure we had food on the table and a roof over our head. Nevertheless, my mother didn't mind letting you know she didn't have a lot of money to spare. I can still hear my mother saying, "Boy I don't got no money for that!" or "I'm broke, don't ask me for no money!"

My mother's side of the family was a little more on the rough, and tough side of the fence. At any given time, our family gatherings could turn into an event filled with fighting, cussing, heavy partying, and yes, tough love. This didn't make me value my mother's side any less, but the experience was different. Our family's issues were not without reason though. My maternal grandmother had a nervous breakdown when my mother was a kid and it affected our family in a huge way. My dad's side of the family was just the opposite of my mother's side. As a family full of singers and musicians, our family gatherings included singing, laughing, and easy loving filled with hugs and kisses all around. However, at times, I never felt like I belonged on either side of my family because I was just different.

I'm the third of four brothers and I was the singer, not very interested in sports except for basketball, always reading, kind of a nerd, and I felt the backlash for it. I was often criticized by family members on my mother's side of the family and on my father's side, my singing just wasn't as a good as the others, or so I felt at the time. I was picked on for being dark-skinned. "Come here black! Boy you look burnt!" my brothers would joke. At the time, it bothered me but I didn't realize I was subconsciously being trained how to think about myself, my world, and my place in it, based on what others thought about me not how I thought about myself. The program was being formed.

Besides telling you all of these detailed and real moments in my life to help you get to know me, I'm also sharing myself with you because I realized that I too was conditioned. Conditioned by others to think a certain way, feel a certain way and see life a certain way. I was influenced and so were you. These influences came not only from family members, but also friends at school, from watching television and music as well.

How we are conditioned as children is something that many never give a second thought to and it's the one thing that affects everything in your life. Know this, you being conditioned without your permission wasn't your choice, but now that you are older, wiser and capable, it's time to examine the conditions and beliefs placed upon your life. It's time to create the life you want! Now don't get me wrong, all conditioning wasn't or isn't bad, but those that hinder you and create self-limiting beliefs can stall you forever.

The History Of The Program

Many of these conditions created mindsets and beliefs in us that we aren't even aware of. From this point on, I'll use the words conditioning and programming interchangeably. See, just like a computer, your mind is also a program. How you think, what you feel, what you believe is all one big program. This program has been built and conditioned in you from birth. In fact, all of those conditions placed on you by others weren't theirs either. For the most part, our parents and grandparents only taught us what was taught to them. You are the program, but you were never designed to be aware of that. All the conditioning and all the habits that were created for you growing up were never meant for you to own them. They simply just were. From generation, to generation, to generation, many of the same ideas, ideologies, feelings and thoughts about life were passed down to you because you were simply the next in line.

I can hear someone saying now, "Well what's wrong with that Antonio? I love my culture, heritage and who I was raised to be." And that's wonderful! There were many great things that happened to me in my childhood too. I love my culture and my heritage too. I'm truly proud of that. But there were also many dark days, scary moments, and beliefs I inherited that don't help who I am today and do not serve me in a positive way.

Surely like day and night, we all have experienced some good and not so good in our childhood.

Changing And Deleting The Program

I have good news! You can change the story of your life. You can change the program, improve the program and yes, even delete the program. You do this by becoming aware. You do this by recognizing those patterns of thought from your childhood and adolescence that have hindered you from truly being in touch with your center. This is the beginning! The power of awareness can never be underestimated.

What is the definition of awareness?

Awareness: Having knowledge and discernment of something

Once you are able to discern the patterns of thought, feelings, and actions that you built from childhood, recognizing that many weren't a result of your own doing, you can change them! My teenage years were filled with feeling of embarrassment of my darker skin tone. I never really realized why I didn't really love myself and the melanin-enriched tone of my skin. I always felt less worthy because of it. It was only when I was able to become aware of all of the negativity that had been fed to me about my skin tone growing up, that I was able to shift my thoughts and feelings about how I look. Now of course you can't remember every little thing that's happened to you as a child or a teenager, but you can remember some of it if you try. You might find this to be a painful process, because many times we shut off pain from our past in order to cope and attempt to move forward. Subconsciously though, we still resonate with that pain or hurt and if you look at your life wholly, you will see the manifestations of that pain. From rejection, to depression, to dishonesty, millions of people around the world are holding on to attributes that they do not desire and would change if they only realized they could.

Creating Your Program:

Here is where the fun can really begin! After you've spent time examining the conditions and programs given to you by others, mentally visualizing yourself getting past them, and affirming that you are able to create the life you want, it's time to actually create the programming *you* want.

In order to create the conditions you want in your life, you must become obsessed, yes, obsessed with them! You must begin to breathe, sleep, and think about what and who you really want to be in life.

Sometimes you don't know what you want but you can feel it. Creating the new program or the new ways of thinking can be exciting! You're stepping into new territory. You're taking control of your destiny, your life, your future. And it can be any way you want it to be. What do you want? I would suggest having a notebook as you travel on your journey throughout this book. This will help you reflect and think through what it is you want with accuracy.

Here are some questions to think about:

What habits did the old conditioning create in me that I'm now changing? What do I want to fulfill in this lifetime before I die? What are some immediate goals I have for myself? What do I want to be, do, or have that the old programming and conditioning prevented me from allowing?

Once you've answered these questions and feel clear in your mind, it's time to move them from inside your head into your actual life:

It may not feel that simple though. Why? Because there is a law in the universe called the law of attraction that you must first learn to master. This law is neither good nor bad. It works according to how you use it.

The law of attraction says that the more you think about something, the more often and easier it becomes for you to think it and bring it to fruition:

Like attracts like. Therefore if you have been focused on negative feelings, perceptions, and the old program for years, it's won't be an overnight transition into this new habit of thought. It's going to take a deliberate, daily commitment to change and do what's best to see the results you want to see. As you are working to create a new program or improve the current one, it's time to raise your awareness of where your focus is most of the time. If you focus on lack, you will get more lack. If you focus on abundance you will get more abundance. Your focus is the key. Your attention to a problem, solution, or anything wanted or unwanted is the key. If you are now aware that the law of attraction is always bringing you more of the program you have built within you, then you now have the power to change it.

Getting Centered Exercise

1. **Find a quiet place to relax.**

2. **Mentally set your intent to use this time to focus only on this mental exercise:** This will aid you in dismissing internal and external distractions. Let your inner self know that you will get back to all those other things in your mind later, but now you are about to focus on this exercise.

3. **Sit down in a comfortable position, close your eyes and take 5-6 slow deep breaths.**

4. **Now begin to think about your childhood:** During this exercise try and visualize yourself when you were younger. What did you need? What were you longing for? What was missing? What were your deepest desires? Hopes? Dreams? Who was there? Who was not there? What pain did that cause?

5. **Now try and see yourself now, as an adult, coming along to comfort that younger you:** Visualize you coming over to your younger self and letting them know, it's all going to be okay. You will be okay. You will survive. You will get through the pain, the hurt. Take a few minutes to really get in touch with this exercise. Maybe you can't see yourself being the comforter but perhaps your spouse, friend, or someone that has touched your life significantly in a powerful positive way can. It might even be an angel or a spiritual-like figure from your religion. Whomever it may be, see them comforting you and helping you realize that everything will be okay and it's okay to release those fears and that pain. Your past does not have to control the decision you make now and who you are now.

6. **After focusing there for a few minutes take a few more deep breaths and allow yourself to truly feel comforted and healed: Open your eyes and repeat these affirmations with deep feeling and conviction:**

a) I am now creating the life I want.
b) I am free.
c) I release and move beyond the pain of my past.

Repeat this exercise as often as needed in order to begin to show yourself that nothing in your past can control you, hold you down, or prevent the amazing future you have ahead of you:

You are free to create today! You are one step closer to living from your center intentionally and more often than ever before.

This now leads us into discussing beliefs:

You are now understanding and realizing more and more how you were conditioned, the effects it has had on you, and you have begun to think about what it is you want to create next in your life. Awareness is key but it isn't enough to effect the kind of change that will literally divert the trajectory of your life toward something greater. For that it will take more. It will take something stronger, more powerful, and key to aligning with your center. It's going to take changing your beliefs.

NOTES

CHAPTER 2

THE CORE

"I believe in my beliefs. Therefore my beliefs are real."

I have this belief that I always bring to the surface of my mind whenever I'm doubting myself, or really need to remember who I am, what I deserve, and the power of my beliefs. Consider the following personal anecdote. A few years ago, my cousin and I were renting an apartment together in the suburbs of Manhattan. It was a nice comfy loft with two cozy furnished rooms and a long modern hallway that connected the two sides. It was perfect for us. She had her space and I had mine. We even had our own entrances into the apartment. Whenever we were aggravated or annoyed with each other she would use her entrance and I would use mine lol. We stayed there for a little over a year until one day I got a call that would change everything. It was a call no one that just moved three thousand miles across the country like I did would want to get. See, we were renting the apartment from a friend of our aunt, who had moved to Atlanta, Georgia but still owned the apartment. I will never forget the day my aunt called me with the news. Ms. Esther had sold the building and we had to be out of the apartment within a month. Yes, you read that correctly. A month. I was devastated!

"A month! Wow really?" I replied. For a few seconds, literally a few seconds, I was nervous, scared and worried all in one. And then, I remember feeling this peace come over me and I reminded myself of why I had moved to New York and my belief that things are always working out for me.

That night I prayed one prayer. I prayed and spoke this prayer one time. One. Time. I believed it with all of my heart and after I finished praying, I did not worry at all about the situation anymore. My prayer was this: I wanted to still live in Harlem no matter what and I wanted to live on the same avenue. I absolutely loved the neighborhood I was living in and my heart was invested there. Harlem has this afro-centric energy that captivated me from day one. I felt at home from the first day.

Fast forward a few days later, I began casually

looking for new places to live. I asked some friends if they knew about any spots that were opening up, and I checked different websites, etc. Mostly, I just waited.

Then a few days after, I felt this intuitive feeling to check craigslist. Yes. Craigslist. Who in the hell checks Craigslist to find apartments anymore right? A man that has to be out of his current apartment within a month. So I'm looking and looking and looking and looking and then I come across this listing for an apartment on the same avenue I was living on, just ten blocks up. It was a Wednesday afternoon and I will never forget it. I quickly reached out to the owner and asked him about the apartment. He got back to me that same night and told me I could come view the apartment the following day, which was a Thursday, or he said, I could come that Friday. I was going to Boston that weekend to visit my uncle, and I knew I could not leave without first going to view this apartment. There was this sense of urgency within me that I had to see this apartment. So I setup an appointment to go view the apartment that Friday evening while I was on break at work. I also didn't work far from where I lived. So perfect right? Anyway, I went to view the apartment and I fell in love instantly. The landlord showed me around, we talked and he told me he had other people that he was also considering and would let me know before the next day. That night, while on the bus to Boston, I got the call that I got the apartment and I could start moving in as soon as I returned from Boston. Wow! I could not believe it. That all happened within a few days of me finding out I had to move. It wasn't hard, I didn't struggle, I simply believed deeply, powerfully and discarded all the negative talk from people and even my own negative thinking that were trying to tell me it would be hard to move.

You have to have unshakable belief! Your belief in your desires affect so much. Even though it may be hard to believe at times, just keep believing. It is unwise to belief in something that prevents your prosperity and greatness. Holding a belief in your mind is what brings results wanted or unwanted.

How Beliefs Are Formed

You are who you are and what you are as result of your beliefs. Your beliefs are a result of your programming and conditioning. Your beliefs rule you. They control what you feel, how you think, and ultimately what you do. Beliefs are so strong and powerful that sometimes you believe things that you don't even realize you believe, mainly because you've believed in them for so long. Did you catch that? So many of your beliefs were ingrained in your mind and heart during those early conditioning days as an infant and adolescent. Beliefs usually are created through repetition. If you tell yourself something long enough, you eventually come to believe it. If your entire childhood you are told you can be anything you want, you soon begin to believe that. You begin to think, feel, and act out of those beliefs. Beliefs are built and become stronger through two things, repetition and conviction. If you repeat a thought over and over to yourself, you soon feel a conviction around it. You become convinced that the belief is real, sooner or later it manifests.

As I mentioned in chapter 1, I was constantly picked on because of my skin tone. As a kid, I didn't understand what was happening to me but what was taking place was the forming of this belief that to be dark skin was to be less than; that I was simply not good enough. This belief led to low self-esteem and problems in other areas of my life. I was social on the outside, but lacking true confidence on the inside. There were even times I wished I could have a lighter complexion. I'm so glad those days are long behind me. I love this chocolate skin now.

What Beliefs Do To Us

What is the definition of belief?
Belief: something that is accepted, considered to be true, or held as an opinion; something believed.

Your beliefs tell you a story about your lives. Your strongest beliefs control your life. You change everything about you when you choose a belief and then allow that belief to set the tone for your life.

How do you come to accept a belief? It happens when you don't challenge a thought, or a condition, or a feeling. When you continue to dwell on it, it often becomes a belief. An unwanted belief is still a belief because you still feel a conviction about it.

Beliefs are things we feel a conviction about or around. These are things that we feel in our soul and in our hearts. Beliefs tell you what to think, what to feel, where to go, what you can and can't do. Your beliefs create everything around you. Now of course, consciously I wouldn't have purposefully created a belief that I wasn't good enough, and that my skin tone was degrading and hideous, but nevertheless I was doing it. I was being conditioned over and over with the same words by the same people and I was creating a belief that did not help me and that I did not like. Have I driven this point about beliefs home? Okay, good.

After Awareness Of Beliefs: Now What?

One of the quickest ways to begin changing an unwanted belief is to be aware of what beliefs you hold that you would like to change. In chapter 1, the exercise of going back to your childhood was all about creating an awareness of what might have been some painful moments you experienced during those years. This exercise helped with creating an awareness in order to move you forward. Creating an awareness does not mean dwelling on bad feelings and thoughts in the past, but it does mean doing your best to figure out what beliefs could be hurting you. Once you can identify a belief, you can choose to change it. You have that power. You must first be aware of it. If you were in a building and it was burning down, you would want to know so you can get out right? Or how about if you were going to work and your typical route was filled with extra traffic because of an accident, you would want to know in advance so you could take a different route if possible right? Same thing with your beliefs. CREATING AWARENESS OF SELF-LIMITING BELIEFS GIVES YOU THE POWER AND THE ABILITY TO CHANGE THEM.

Changing Old Beliefs

Now on the other hand, if you use all of your energy to focus on changing old beliefs you won't make a change. The key is to not try and change old beliefs once you are aware of them but to focus on creating new ones. All of your mind's power has to be focused on creating new beliefs and disregarding the old ones. Remember earlier we talked about the law of attraction? If you are fighting old thoughts, you are actually making them bigger and giving them a stronger foundation to build pathways to similar thoughts. Conserve all your energy for creating new beliefs.

Here are some examples of some possible old beliefs people often hold unto.

Old belief: I'm not good enough (This is from the previous conditioning and programming, and yes it can change!)

New desired belief: I'm more than enough and I am loved.

Old belief: I'm not talented and earning money is so hard.

New Belief: I am extremely creative and I find and create ways for abundance.

Getting Centered Exercise

Answer the following questions with honesty and deep thought:

1. What do I believe about myself that could be preventing me from receiving my desires and accomplishing my goals?

2. What do I believe about others that could be hurting me?

3. What do I believe about the world that's not good?

4. Do my beliefs align with my actions that I take toward my goals?

Affirmations: Finish the sentences below with powerful positive statements about good beliefs you hold or hope to belief.

Practice and read these affirmations five times when you wake up and five times before going to sleep (Even more often if you want).

a) **I believe *I am*...**
b) **I love believing...**
c) **I am now choosing to be...**

NOTES

CHAPTER 3

IT'S THE THOUGHT THAT COUNTS

D o you truly understand the power of your thoughts? Do you really understand the power that your thinking has? The way you think about everything and how you think about it has created the life you are living now. It does not matter how you came to the conclusion of those thoughts, it only matters that you actually are thinking those thoughts with a deep-seated belief.

Every second, of every minute, of every day, you are thinking. You are thinking about something. Whether it's "Damn I hope that dog didn't poop on my couch!" or "If she is cheating on me I'm leaving her!" or maybe even "I can't wait to get off work. I hate this place." No matter what, we are always thinking. Thinking is energy. It can literally cause physical reactions in your body such as sadness, happiness, depression, and anxiety.

Now pause. Before I continue I've got to let this be known right now:

Public Service Announcement

Your thoughts are creating your life! Now you might be sitting back saying to yourself, *I know this already.* And I'm sure you do, but there are many things we know that we don't utilize to get the greatest results we want out of life. Your thoughts create habits. And those habits are either helping you build the life you want or creating the life you don't want.

How Thoughts Come To You

Have you ever been sitting in a room with someone or a group of people and perhaps you were thinking a thought or thinking about a song and someone else in the room said what you were thinking? Or they started singing the song you were thinking about? It's not by accident. Some people call this mental telepathy, others say it's random. The *Journal of Consciousness Studies* speaks on topics similar to this and research as well.

One thing is for sure, thoughts are extremely powerful. I've always felt that sometimes thoughts float in the air, many times from one person to another and we don't even know it. Sometimes you create thoughts based on what you are watching or what you are listening to. Other times your thoughts come from, well, things that you've believed in for a very long time. Those thoughts helps to create even more thoughts like the ones you already are thinking. In any case, thoughts are powerful and they bring into your life wanted things or unwanted things. It all depends on how much attention you are giving to certain thoughts and how much feeling you put behind it.

I'll never forget when I first decided to move to New York. It really all began when I was twelve years old, more precisely, it was December 27th, 2002. It was my first time visiting New York and my aunt brought me to the Empire State Building. I remember waiting hours and hours to get to the top. Once there, it was the most beautiful thing I had ever seen. The city lights, the tall, immaculate buildings, the sirens of traffic below and the crisp cold air. Well the crisp cold air wasn't my favorite thing, but still, it added to the Christmas feeling in the air. It was the power of the moment. Right then and there, I declared, "I'm going to live in this city one day!" I knew it for sure. I knew it without a doubt. I knew it with such clarity. That thought came to me often, and it came with strong positive feelings. Nothing was going to stop me from fulfilling that desire or embracing that thought. In that moment my thoughts were working for me. Different experiences can cause you to have different thoughts, the key is believing in the thoughts that enhance your well-being and positive aspects.

Positive Patterns of Thinking

After that day, I kept the thought of moving to New York in the back of mind. Throughout middle school and especially high school, I would ponder on it every now and then. In college I began thinking about it more and by my junior year, I was thinking on it heavily. I knew there were obstacles I would face, but it really didn't matter because I'd created a powerful positive thought with a strong feeling that I believed. New York was already my home in my mind. And doubt didn't stand a chance at stopping me. No way. No how.

A thought alone isn't enough though. You must create a pattern of thoughts about a particular thing or topic. It is not merely enough to think about something once or every blue moon and think you will begin to manifest that thought or desire into your life. I'd created a pattern of thoughts and beliefs around a desire I wanted and today I'm living that desire. I'm living in New York and doing what I love to do!

Negative Thought Patterns

In the same way you can think something positively for a long period of time with strong feeling and manifest it, you can also do the opposite. A thought pattern isn't based on anything other than consistent engagement in the same kind of thoughts, positive or negative. Negative thoughts however don't feel good. You can tell they aren't good for you because they don't feel good. It's just like if you try and touch a hot stove or stick your finger on a sharp nail, instantly you will be able to tell that, hey, I probably shouldn't touch that stove or that hot nail. And you'll stop. For some reason, you don't seem to notice or think about your thoughts in the same way. You allow negative thought patterns to linger, thoughts about fear, pain, disappointment, hurt, grief, and anger. These thoughts soon produce correlating experiences in your lives that we don't want.

Justified In Negative Thought Patterns

Now here is where it gets tricky. Often times you may feel that you are justified in feeling what you feel. You may be angry at someone, or maybe you received a terrible diagnosis from your doctor. Perhaps you're going through a divorce and you feel like you should feel depressed during that transition. Many people would say, you are allowed to feel depressed, you are going to grieve, and that's okay. Don't worry, I'm no different. I think that when something that we don't desire appears in our lives, we will have an initial shock or fear towards it. It's part of the human experience. I am not saying you will never think any negative thoughts or have a negative thought pattern. In fact when you do get caught up in a negative thought pattern, it still benefits you because once you can come out of it or realize you are in it, the greater your desire will be for something different. What I am saying is you don't want it to become a negative thought pattern that you begin to think about daily. With those negative thoughts comes strong and lasting negative feelings which will most likely get worse. At least at first.

Do The Opposite

Knowing the power of thoughts and thought patterns, you want to turn your attention to do exactly the opposite. And you do this by thinking thoughts that you want to think not thoughts that you feel you have to think. Or thoughts based on what's happening right now. Think about the many people that have faced obstacles and challenges in life but overcame them. It's not easy but they first had to start with the right mindset. It's not comfortable at first but it's doable. And you begin to see the results in your life! The law of mental action, which is a universal law that says we get what we think about often and the most. Turn your thoughts around and you will turn your life around too! It's a simple concept but extremely powerful if you give it a try and commit to doing it on various issues in your life.

Listen Without Judgement

Because of thought patterns, you can find yourself automatically thinking something without much effort. If every time you go to a restaurant, they take a long time with serving your food and that is the experience you focus on, your thought pattern around restaurants and food may become that this is a long arduous process. Now you may no longer intentionally be thinking the thought every single time you step into a restaurant, but in a sort of habitual way, the thought just appears and gives you automatic responses. It may be a general belief you now hold about restaurants. A very powerful thing to become aware of is how your thoughts work against you. When you are with people, or at work, begin to notice what thoughts instantly pop up in your head. Notice what you pay attention to. As you are listening to these thoughts, listen to them as if you were standing outside your body or as if you were another person listening to them. Listen without judgement. Don't beat yourself up for noticing negative thought patterns. In fact, get excited.

That awareness benefits you like nothing else. It allows you to finally say, "Gotcha! You ole nasty no good thoughts. No more. No more dwelling on you. I'm going to begin to do something different." Now that is your power! You have options. Listen to and change what's being thought of.

Think On What You Want

What you give your attention to the most always manifests in your life. Also, your thoughts are being heard by a universal intelligence (God, or whatever you would like to call the magnificent power that lives within all of us). The thoughts you constantly think act as signals that you want more of what you're focused on despite those thoughts being negative or positive. So guess what? Always let your purest intention be to move your thoughts toward the success you want and to leave out thoughts about things you don't want. This isn't easy but it can be if it becomes your gentle, daily, effort to do. Not trying too hard to think on what you want, but in a pleasant, soft way, redirecting your thoughts toward what you want instead of what you don't want. Universal intelligence will begin to respond to your beliefs and your thoughts, guaranteed! You were born with great abilities to focus your life into what you want it to be and there is no limit on what you can become. It's time you be reminded, that that time is now!

Positive Self-Talk

You are with yourself all day. You are thinking thoughts all day. It's vital that you create positive self-talk with yourself! It doesn't matter what's happening in your life. This will benefit you in any situation. Any. It's not you denying or faking anything. Instead, it's you caring about what comes into your life, and therefore being deliberate about monitoring and managing it. If you really want to improve your life, you've got to have positive self-talk. It's the conversation with self that matters most and that also affects what happens to you. Practice these sayings:

"You're doing well, keep going."

"I am so proud of me, because no matter what, I am not giving up."

"I know I don't see it happening for me yet, and I still feel some doubt but that's okay I'm going to keep taking action on my goals and dreams."

"I know I'm frustrated but this all is temporary. I'll figure it out."

Find a way to make yourself feel better, no matter what. In the next chapter we'll discuss what having positive self-talk creates in you and how to make sure you are focused on that no matter what.

It's time you were aligned with what really matters the most to you. Your Center!

REMEMBER: THE MORE YOU THINK ABOUT WHAT YOU WANT AND FEEL GOOD WHILE DOING IT, THE MORE YOU ARE INVITING WHAT YOU WANT INTO YOUR LIFE!

Getting Centered Exercise

Answer the following questions with honesty and deep thought:

1. What thought patterns have I created that are not helping me in life?

2. What thought patterns about my life would I like to create?

3. Think of something you want to become, something you really want accomplish in life and then:

   a) Act and believe as if it would be impossible to not receive or become what you are asking for.

   b) Only think heavily about what you want to be or a goal you have when it feels good to think about it.

   c) Stop thinking about it when it feels like you are focused on the lack of it.

NOTES

CHAPTER 4

THE CENTER

All Roads Lead Here

Imagine you are driving a car. Your thoughts are the steering wheel. Your beliefs are the tires. And *your center* is the engine. What is the center you ask? Your center is that inner part of you that is your soul and essentially your spirit. It is the spiritual part of you. It's the place where your power and purpose truly align. It's the place where the universe takes whatever you are putting out with your energy and gives it back to you. Your center can be defined as the seat of your soul.

In essence, your center connects you to your deepest, truest, and most dominant feelings. We talked about programming, beliefs, and managing our thoughts in previous chapters and those things matter absolutely. However, your beliefs and your thoughts have no power if there is no center behind them! When someone compliments you or you see someone you really love and you get a rush of excitement through your body, that's you feeling your center. It's the place of love, peace, and clarity. On the one hand, when you allow certain beliefs and thoughts that hinder you to take over your center, you can feel the disconnection because you feel awful. It doesn't feel good.

Here are some basic examples....

Thought: I'm never going to make it in life.
Feelings of: Sadness, hopelessness, fear.

Thought: I hate this job. I'm always so tired and I never have time for me.
Feelings: negativity, discouragement, frustration, annoyed.

Thought: I know I can figure it out some way. I know I can!
Feelings: optimistic, cheerful, confident, inspired.

Almost immediately, you can become aware of when you are not aligned with your center vs. when you are.

What You Feel You Make Real

Growing up and not having my father around to support me, to love me and to guide me on this journey of becoming a young man kept me from aligning with my center for years. Every time you think a thought with strong feeling behind it, you can feel if you are aligned with your center or if you're not. Every time I thought about my father and the disappointment and the hurt that came with it, it was clear to see, I was not in alignment with my center. Your center, your deepest truest self is always pointed to love because that's who you are! I'm a lover and so are you. When you don't feel that love, that joy, that peace, that hopefulness, you are not aligned with your center no matter what the circumstance may be!

Feeling Habits

If you can grasp this concept and become more aware of your feeling habits, your life could begin to change forever. A feeling habit is just that: a habitual way of feeling about something or someone that you've built up over time. Now check this out, habits that make you feel good, increase your productivity, and get you the results you want are habits you should continue. Habits that make you feel terrible, decrease your productivity, and create results you don't want are habits you don't want to continue. Always remember you do have the power to change!

As I mentioned earlier, it starts with being aware. It starts with noticing what you feel in different situations and circumstances and adjusting your mood to how you *want* to feel versus how you don't want to feel.

Here is where some usually go wrong in this process. You might feel justified in feeling negative emotions such as worry or hurt concerning whatever the situation is and you could be right. What you must consider though is that it might be a feeling habit you've created over time that needs to be changed! Not only that, you want it to change! That's if you want to move toward all the great things in your life. Consistent negative feeling habits can slow down all the well-being and good that has your name on it. Is it worth it?

A Magnificent Realization

Feeling habits may have controlled you before, but now it's time you took control of them. It's time to take your power back!

You can deliberately, with practice, learn to control what you feel about any and everything. Isn't that wonderful to know? Don't you like knowing that? I can hear someone right now going, "Yeah, yeah, yeah, blah, blah, blah, easier said than done." And I say to you, it's only easier said than done because you're saying it's easier said than done, and it's something you weren't really taught before and something you probably don't practice often. Did you learn how to ride a bike the first time you tried? When you were a baby did you start walking the very first time you tried? No! You tried and tried and tried and failed, and tried again, until you began to master those skills. It's the same thing with your emotions. Once you can accept that you can control what you feel unconditionally, than you're well on your way to being in touched with your center. Your center is your connection to the greatest power that is, universal intelligence. Your center is divine. Your center is your inner-being that guides you, loves you, and supports you. Your center is ready to give you what you desire at any moment but you've got to be ready for it. You become ready for it by practicing positive feelings, positive thoughts, and positive beliefs.

I keep referencing my father throughout the book because his life heavily affected mine. For years and years, I held strong resentment toward my dad. I love him dearly, always have and always will but, it was simply too hard to let him off the hook for not being around when I was growing up. Quite frankly, him still not being around as I got older still bothered me. It's one of the most challenging and uncomfortable feelings to love someone but yet have resentment toward them. This was uncomfortable because my true center is *only* about love. Resentment, bitterness, and unforgiveness are nowhere near the vibration and energy of love I carry. Eventually, I had to come to the conclusion that me holding resentment was like me holding a powerful weapon against myself. It's like taking a sword or a knife and stabbing yourself with it because in actuality, you're the one feeling the greatest pain. Not only was I feeling pain, it was beginning to spread into other areas of my life. My father and I now are building a beautiful and healthy relationship.

Be Patient

Upon realizing you can deliberately guide your feelings and thoughts to what you want, it might feel exciting, overwhelming, and damn right impossible. Be patient with yourself. You must remember you are facing years of old thought patterns and feeling habits that have more than likely kept you from receiving and seeing life fully from your center. Be consistent and gentle with yourself. Expect to see the results you want from guiding your emotions to your desires. Sometimes, even until this day, I am tested with old hurt, and old pains that try and return. It's a daily task of recentering myself and reminding myself that I've grown, matured and don't have to feel that way anymore and to remember what I know now! No matter what happens, no matter what comes back up from your past....

YOU SHOULD ALWAYS REMEMBER THAT YOUR PAST FEELINGS DO NOT HAVE TO DETERMINE YOUR FUTURE FEELINGS OR YOUR CURRENT FEELINGS!

Identify It

As exciting as it is to deliberately guide your emotions and feelings and watch your life begin to change to what you desire for it to be, understand that you cannot completely obliterate negative emotions. Experiencing negative emotions has its benefits as well.

Imagine your feelings being like a GPS. When you are feeling good, you are going in the right direction and when you are feeling anger, bitterness, or other strong negative emotions you are not. Point blank period. It doesn't matter the reason. When you realize you are going in the wrong direction, what do you do? You find a way to begin turning in the right direction. It might take a while because you might be on a one way street or you might be on the highway but the point is, you find a way to turn around and get moving in the right direction. Negative emotion means one thing and one thing only; I am not aligned with my center and I am limiting all the wonderful things that may be trying to enter into my life. Negative emotions are actually good because they help you be aware of what you are doing with your energy. If you are trying to create the life you want and not a life that you settle for, you should feel strong gratitude and appreciation for that awareness. That awareness is guidance, and it is important. That knowing is part of your power. Negative emotion is just a signal to do something different or move in a different direction.

Whatever You Do, Don't Do This

Let's take it back to that analogy about imagining your feelings being like a GPS. Once you realize that you are going in the wrong direction, you might get frustrated with yourself, and angry thinking, "Damn. I can't believe I've been going in the wrong direction all this time. What the heck ugh!" This response is understandable depending on how long you've been going in the wrong direction, and if you're rushing or trying to get somewhere important. Beating yourself up will not help you get out of the traffic faster. Remind yourself of this and say these words:

"I can always begin by finding a way to turn around."

Once you have that moment of realization that you're going in the wrong direction and you might be upset and angry about it, you always start to turn to go in the right direction and that's what matters most! This is the same way you have to be when it comes to negative emotions. Do your best to stop or change the feeling the moment it tries to rise in you. When you stop that momentum from building, it will feel good. It will feel like you are in control, because you are. When you realize and feel those negative emotions rising up in you like a flame being ignited, you begin to do something different! And notice how all of a sudden, the diagnosis, the hurt, or the disappointment, don't seem so bad. This means that life has begun to attract to you a better feeling, which brings the better situation, which brings the better outcome. Try it and notice what happens.

Getting Centered Exercise

1. **Think about and visualize how you want to feel in a particular situation you would like to improve your feeling habit around:** See the situation play out in your mind. How does it feel? What does it do to your body and mind? Leave out the circumstance of how it currently is and *only* focus on how you *want* it to be no matter what!

2. **Begin to walk, talk and live as if how you want it to be is your truth:** Interact with it as if it's not only in your imagination, but that it's real the way you see it, because it is. Do your best to turn your attention from what you've been doing and feeling and work on expanding your desired feelings for that outcome.

NOTES

CHAPTER 5

DREAMING AGAIN

**Who would you be if you hadn't been
programmed?**

In the beginning of the book we talked about
how we all were conditioned without our
permission. How everything you learned and
was taught at birth had absolutely nothing to do
with you picking it consciously. But dammit not
anymore right? When you begin to wake up every
single day thinking good thoughts, feeling good
feelings and holding good beliefs, nothing and no
one can keep you from anything. When you begin
to consciously take over the program in your head,
it's like a veil being lifted from your eyes and you
begin to see the world for what it really is. A
beautiful place filled with absolute wonder. You
begin to create life instead of just letting life
happen to you. Now that you understand what
your center is and that it's the place of all

inspiration, all love, all joy, all abundance, it's time to tap into it! So far in this book, we've talked extremely generally. But in order to create a life you want, you've got to focus into your center, feel good and start getting specific. Getting specific can get tricky so you must make sure you're setup for success first. Are you ready?

What do you really want in life?

This is where it can get tricky, sticky and straight up challenging. But this is where it really gets good too! It's time to really specifically think about what you want. Here is what I mean:

General: I want my life to turn out good.

Specific: I want my life to turn out with me being a top executive for MTV making 200k with three kids and being a New York Times best-selling author by the time I'm forty.

Do you see the difference? Being general is good. You want to be general when you don't know exactly what you want or need in life but you know that it has to be something better than what you have now. When you can't seem to get to what your life would look like in specific terms, it's okay to start off thinking generally. When you begin to get into the trend of being generally positive, you must increase your faith to learning how to become specifically positive.

Remember that tricky part I mentioned? Yeah. This is it. Getting specific is not always easy because many times you haven't given thought to what you truly want. And why? It's because the program you were taught which was engrained in you was what others wanted for you, not necessarily what you want for yourself.

I remember I had a friend in college that studied architecture his first three years and then in his senior year he switched his major. My first was reaction was "Wow, you've got to be kidding me." I couldn't believe after three years of studying, paying tuition, and so much time passing, that he was willing to change his major so abruptly. But once he told me why it all made sense. See for my friend Kevin, he'd been programmed by his parents that he needed to pursue a career that paid well. Like becoming a doctor, a lawyer, an engineer, or an architect. So, just to please his parents, he did just that. For three long years he lived and studied something he really didn't have any passion for. It wasn't until that fourth year that he finally realized, *I've got to do this for me.*

It's time you do the same! It's time you get specific about your dreams and desires. Keyword, *your* dreams and desires. What do you really want? Not what do you think you can have, but what do you really and truly want? For some, the programming at birth conditioned them in a way that makes the process of figuring themselves out can be cloudy and challenging, but it doesn't have to be. And if it is for you, knowing that you can change this is more than enough to get you on your way to realizing what it is you really want in life.

The program that you were given or taught at birth, usually doesn't allow you to focus on what you want, but more so on what others desire for you or their views of you.

Visualizing Your Dreams NOW!

So just how do you start the journey of being specific? How do you begin to get specific enough so that you can be aligned with your center to live your best life now? A great tool to use is visualization. I've always believed that if you can see it in your mind, then that is the first step to creating it. Seeing it in your mind is a wonderful way to set up a powerful vision for what you want specifically.

See It, Feel It, Believe it

Your vision must be so strong and so real to you that it moves you to the action that changes your life. That is how you know that you have truly begun to create the life and the vision you want for yourself. How do you know you really believe it? Watch what you do, watch what you say and watch what you think. All three must be the same and aligned with your center. If you say I visualized me opening up a restaurant and having one of the best food chains in town, but you don't put in the time and the effort to get it done, you really don't believe it. I can hear someone saying, "What? Are you serious? You can't tell me I don't really believe in my dreams and goals and desires. I do."

But here is where it gets tricky, many times we may want things but it doesn't mean we believe we can have what we want. Our actions will always validate what we believe. It's not what we say only, it's what we do.

Example:

Saying: I am prosperous and the universe provides of me!

Thinking: I don't have enough.

Feeling: Nervous, and fearful about losing it all.

That is an example of not being aligned with your center. What you're saying, feeling and thinking must be one. It must be so closely put together that it moves you into action. Here is an example of the opposite:

Saying: I am prosperous.

Feeling: I have abundance.

Thinking: I have more than enough.

You see the difference? Wow! All three are lined up and are in sync. When you've got all three lined up, you're going to be turning your dreams into reality. You've got the formula for success. You've made the crossover from doubt and fear to belief and power. Now nothing can keep you from your center.

THE CENTER | 67

Getting Centered Exercise

1. **Write down a time you will personally take out to visualize the life you want and when you will do it each day (8-10 minutes):** Do your best to not waver from these two specific time periods. Set your intent for this exercise that you are putting this time aside for you to get specific about your desires, goals, and dreams. This is serious business and you are not playing around.

2. **Get a pen and paper and begin writing down a plan, a detailed plan for your desired life:** What does it feel like? What does it look like? Heck, you can even write what you think it will smell like. What city are you living in? What organization are you running? Are you married? Do you have children? What do your children look like? How does your relationship feel? These are only some of a handful of questions you can begin asking yourself. You aren't focused on the how you are simply focused on what you want.

3. **After writing down your vision, get into a relaxed position and start to feel yourself taking deep breaths:** Begin to visualize everything you wrote out. The fact that you already wrote it out helps your mind to accept it even faster. Visualize it just how you wrote it. Visualize it and believe that it is possible. Visualize the touches, the places, the things, the character and personality you'll have and everything in between. You can do it. It's your life and your vision.

4. **After you have finished creating the vision in your mind, release it and trust that the universe is bringing it to pass:** Do not revert back. Do not be tricked into going back to an old vision or doubting yourself or what you see. If you can see it, you can create it in real life. It's all up to you. You have the power.

5. **Create a vision board that represents your strongest feelings, desires and thoughts about your vision:** Use this vision board daily to keep you inspired and looking forward to what's next.

6. **Trust that what you want and what you see is yours:** Don't look to others who don't know it, who can't see it, and who don't believe it. I want you to know it's real so matter-of-factly that you are living it before you are living it.

7. **Realize that living from your center is the beginning of you living a great life that's unconditional, but will bring the conditions you desire:** Don't search for the condition outside of you, feel them inside of you first. See it in your mind and in your heart and watch what comes to pass. I know I keep saying this but, yes, this is where it really gets *good*! It's time to apply what you know deliberately.

NOTES

CHAPTER 6

GET A MOVE ON IT!

When I was twelve years old, my aunt took me to the top of the Empire State Building. It was Christmas day, and my birthday was also two days later; I was in heaven. It was the first of many things for me. It was the first time I'd seen snow. It was the first time I'd ever been to New York City, and it was the first time I'd ever been to the top of the Empire State Building. I remember that day so vividly because it was a day that changed my life. I had on a yellow and blue sweat suit that my mother bought me for my birthday, and I felt fly as hell.

We'd waited three hours just to get all the way up to the top of the Empire State Building, and once there, overlooking the beauty that is New York City, I remember thinking to myself, *I've never seen or felt anything like this.* It was an instant love connection with a breathtaking view and city that my soul could not deny.

Right then and there, I knew I was going to move to New York City. I said it to myself in my head. *I'm going to live here!* There was no doubt in my heart or mind that this was the city I belonged in. I felt a connection. It felt like home. It would be eleven years later when at the age of twenty-three, two weeks before my twenty-fourth birthday, I did it. I moved to the city of my dreams. I remember the day I left for the airport thinking, *Now I am starting my life!* It felt right. It was right.

Follow That Feeling

Between those eleven years from the age of twelve to twenty-three, I would occasionally think about New York. My mindset was always *yep, I'm going to live there one day.* I didn't know the when, nor the how. All I had was my belief! All I had was my knowing. I also knew I wasn't going to make a move until it felt right. Until I felt within me, this is the time to go.

The point of that anecdote is this, once you align with your center, everything starts to change! You begin to get impulses; you begin to know what to do and when to do it. You start getting these ideas and intuitive inclinations where you know what to do next. You know it's time for a change or time to leave that job or move out or whatever it may be for you. You simply know.

What am I saying? Inspired action is the best action! When you feel inspiration to do something, to build something, to go somewhere, to call someone, here is my advice. DON'T IGNORE THAT! Yes, I'm shouting it to you. I'll do it again to really drive my point. DON'T IGNORE THAT FEELING! That feeling is powerful. That feeling of inspiration to act is leading you toward something wonderful that you have been asking for, needing to know, or that simply will help you along your journey. Don't take it for granted. True guidance within you can always be felt. It always feels like you can do the thing you feel you need to do. When you align with your center, you don't have to push yourself to go after your dreams and desires, your dreams and desires push you. One is like hard work and the latter is more like oneness with your purpose, alignment with your center. Feel the difference? Let's continue on.

The Old You and Minor Setbacks

What I'm writing about is something many people do not realize or are not aware of that happens to them. Sometimes people get all excited when they read books like this because they make you feel good, and they should. However, you must be careful of the old systems and programs that will definitely try and creep back in.

So you're on your journey, you're aligned with your center and you think, *Damn, this feels good. I know what to do, when to do it, and I am ready for the next thing.* Lo and behold, the old you has other plans. The old you that was out of touch with your center is not just going down without a fight. The old you has been dominating your mind, actions and energy for a long time. Now you are ready to change? Trust me, you will get some push back from your own self, but the difference is now you will be prepared. You will recognize that old self trying to come back and you will be able to stop it right away. You will be ready because you will be enjoying thriving from your center!

YOU MUST BE AWARE OF THE OLD YOU TRYING TO SABOTAGE THE NEW YOU!

It's inevitable and it will happen. Why? Because everything you have ever lived is still in your mind. You have something called memory, and your memory of your past can often try and take you back, but you must declare, I AM NOT GOING

BACK! I am not going back to my old ways, to my old thoughts, and to my old habits. Occasionally, you will. You will slip into old thought habits and feeling habits, but now knowing about your center and how to connect with it, you're unstoppable and the universe (or Jesus, Yahweh, The Eternal Now, Buddha, The Great Spirit, etc. whatever floats your boat) has your back.

Don't see the old you trying to creep back in as an enemy of self. It's just the way it was for so long, and it's natural for there to be a little or a lot of resistance to change. Here are the thoughts you want to have when facing a minor setback or even a MAJOR one:

"It's ok, I've been here before, but this time I know what to do."

"I am figuring it out moment by moment, one moment at a time."

"I'm not the same person I was before. I'm better now."

"I didn't expect to change without making mistakes; after all, I am still learning and growing."

"I feel good knowing there are areas I still need to work on and I'm okay with that."

"I can always realign with my center no matter what. It's what's there for me."

The best way to handle setbacks is to know they are going to push you even further once you get past them. Trust the process. Love yourself. Critique yourself but do not criticize yourself. You deserve all the love and affection. It will prosper you in ways you can't imagine. When setbacks happen, use the self-talk thoughts above and similar ones to remind yourself you are powerful, loved, incredible, and moving forward not backwards! Try this process and watch what happens.

It's Time to Evaluate

When I sat down to start writing this book, I needed to know what this book was going to do for me and for others. I needed to know why I wanted to write this book and why people would care to read it. Your why in life is everything! When you know your why, it propels you forward in the mist of adversity, setbacks, doubts, and fears. Nothing can stop a person who is convinced of their why and keeps it at the forefront of their mind to achieve success and stay aligned with their center.

It's not always easy though. As I stated in chapter 1, when we were programmed at birth, we didn't have a why as to the religion we were subjected to or the places we went or even the people we entertained. Initially, our why was chosen for us. Why do you want to be wealthy? Why do you want to have good health? Why do you want to start that organization? These are not only prominent questions you need to ask yourself, they are vital.

As you ask yourself these types of questions, it causes you to dive deep into the inner recesses of your heart, soul and mind for the answers. You begin to realize that you deserve more. You begin to push past your fears and worries because you are motivated and inspired by your why.

One of the reasons I wanted to go far away, and I do mean far away, from home for college was because I knew I deserved a chance to create a life that I truly wanted. Being at home and trying to go to college was not going to work. When I say home, I mean living in the city I was raised in. The noise of family members telling me what they think I should do or what I should study or family drama, it would have all been huge distractions. Another why for me was a chance to learn more about me with just myself; allowing me to discover my center more often. Being in a new atmosphere would allow that and it did. So what is your why?

As you are thinking about your why, for a little while, focus on your life long-term. Being aligned with your center is something you want to master throughout your life. It's simply up to you to choose to decide that you can align with it and shift your focus to letting that be the most important thing you do. Aligning with your center is one thing. Learning to live there is another. You want to live life from your center, it's the best life, it's the life you were born to live. Go ahead and complete the Getting Centered Exercises below. You'll be happy you did.

Getting Centered Exercise

1. **Repeat these affirmation with feeling and conviction:**
   I AM not discouraged by my setbacks.
   I AM taking massive inspirational action toward my dreams.

2. **Write down 5 positive feelings you get when you take inspired action and see results.**

3. **Practice following your intuition:** Look for moments where you hear the voice inside of you telling you to call someone or go to a certain store or read a certain book. Often these intuitive moments are leading us toward something we desire and can aide us in our next action step toward our goals and dreams.

4. **Write a letter to yourself about your why:** Why you plan to be centered more often and why you want to accomplish the specific dream and goals you have for yourself in life.

NOTES

CHAPTER 7

THERE IS POWER IN THIS

Being connected to your center is your greatest power. It is not something that you have to fight to do when you realize your center is the real you. It is the connection to everything you desire to be, do, and have in life. As you learn to harness the power within you, focusing from your center gets easier over time. Many people think, feel and take action from their center more than they realize. All of the great singers, actors and actresses, athletes, scientist, teachers, etc. They all accomplish greatness because they thrive from their center.

I Wake Up Like This

How you start your day matters. It matters because how you start your day sets the tone for your day. One of the first things I do each morning is meditate. I meditate anywhere from five to fifteen minutes and it literally makes me feel empowered and prepared for whatever the day may bring. After meditation, one thing is for sure, I feel connected with my center. Meditation is sure way to reconnect with your center every single time. You can't just meditate for one day though and expect to see a drastic change in your life. In the same way you can't hit the gym once every three months and expect to stay in shape. Let's take a moment and talk about the power of meditation.

What is Meditation?

Definition according to Yoga International: Meditation is a precise technique for resting the mind and attaining a state of consciousness that is totally different from the normal waking state. It is the means for fathoming all levels of ourselves and finally experiencing the center of consciousness within.

Something I've noticed many people say happens when they meditate or attempt to is that they can't seem to quiet their mind. *"My mind won't shut up! I can't do that meditation stuff. I've tried it before; it's too hard."* What I want you to realize is that meditation isn't always you quieting your mind.

Imagine you were in a movie theater and all your thoughts began scrolling across the screen. In meditation, this could possibly be how it is. There are a variety of ways to meditate. Each individual finds what way works best for them. I would encourage you to research different styles that might work for you. For me, I love guided visualization meditation. In guided visualization meditation, I'm usually listening to some type of audio that is encouraging relaxing and positive experiences. Guided visualization audio can have a variety of focuses including gratitude, love, peace, and success. I absolutely love listening to The Honest Guys on YouTube. Their meditations are soothing and relaxing.

Sometimes I meditate to receive clarity and sometimes I receive clarity as a result of meditation. There have been countless times that I've felt drained at work, stressed over a family issue, frustrated or worried over something, only to realize meditation is what begins to change everything. You can meditate in your car, at home, on the train, or anywhere where you can have a few minutes alone to get still and focus within.

There is also tons of research studies done on meditation. I won't go into all of them because this isn't a book on meditation, but I will share one finding. Dr. Norman Rosenthal of the David Lynch Foundation discovered that people who practice meditation are 30 percent less likely to die from heart disease. This study was published in the journal *Circulation: Cardiovascular Quality and Outcomes*. The participants were asked to take a class focused on a type of meditation called transcendental meditation.

Mosby's Medical Dictionary defines transcendental meditation as:

A psychophysiological exercise designed to lower levels of tension and anxiety and increase tolerance of frustration. TM has been described as a state of consciousness that does not require any physical or mental control. During meditation, the person enters a hyper-metabolic state in which there is reduced activity of the adrenergic component of the autonomic nervous system.

Over a five year time period, the participants experienced a 48 percent reduction in the risk of heart attack, stroke, and death. Feel free to research other incredible findings about meditation as well.

Connectedness

So how do you stay connected to your center? How do you know when you aren't connected to your center? Well again, you know you're connected to your center because you feel inspired, lively, and like you know what the next step in life is for you or on a smaller scale, the immediate next step. Disconnection from your center is the opposite. You don't feel spiritually supported from within. It's uncomfortable and lonely. It feels off because it is. *Wait huh?* I can hear someone saying that to themselves. *Well, Antonio, I do feel inspired, but I still don't know what to do next. I don't know if I should stay in the relationship or if I should quit my job or move to that new city.*

And what I beg to differ is that you do know, you just haven't realized what you know. Sometimes you know and you're afraid of what you know. Don't be. It's a good thing. The great thing about being focused within your center is that you realize more about what you want in life at deeper levels.

What I'm actually saying is; trust the process and simply take the next action step that feels right. If you haven't got the entire thing figured out then move on to whatever it is that does feel right. See here is something I want you to know, when you don't feel good or you feel lost, or fearful, your center is still there for you. Your center still sits within you already knowing what the next step is or what great potential you have. It simply takes you concentrating on that to tap into it. So what am I really saying? When you are one with your center, you can simply follow what you feel the next step is to get to the answers you are searching for.

Don't Force it, Feel it and Visualize.

Being immersed with your center is not something that is supposed to laborious. You should never feel like you are fighting to get aligned with your center because once you start doing that, you begin to associate being aligned with your center with really hard work. Being at one with your center is about ease, it's about love, it's about being in a flow, and most importantly, it's about focus! It's about allowing, not forcing. You can look at all that appears to be going wrong or all that is going right. It's totally up to you.

The actor Jim Carrey, you do know him, right?

From the film, *Dumb and Dumber* and *The Mask*, a legendary comedian and actor. Years ago, on The Oprah Winfrey Show, he talked about how when he was broke and nowhere near as successful as he is now, he was roaming the streets of L.A. Carrey talked about how he would visualize the life he wanted. He would begin to visualize him getting calls from directors, being in films he wanted to be in and really living his dreams. He spoke about how all of this did one thing; it made him feel better. He also mentioned on the show how he wrote himself a check for ten million dollars and put it in his wallet; giving himself three to five years to make that exact amount of money. Once again, he was broke, and all visualizing did was make him feel better. Exactly three years later, after walking around with that check in his wallet the entire time, he received a ten million dollar check for the film, *Dumb and Dumber*. When you truly align with your center, it feels good and it brings marvelous results! All it takes is a willingness to discard everything else and simply feel the joy of what you want and allow it to be. Now, of course, he did work too; going out and seeking opportunities, but it was what he did prior to that work that set him up for success. That is why he is so successful. We'll talk more about inspired action ahead.

Gratitude Power

If more people knew about the wonderful power of gratitude, they would complain less and they would do it intentionally. Using your mind to look for gratitude is not only good, it brings good results for you and to you as well. The power of gratitude is that life begins to show you more things to be grateful for. You feel honored and privileged to be who you are, to be in the space that you're in and to be living the life you are living because it's an opportunity to live.

Desperation Repels, Gratitude Attracts

Now, I must be very clear about something. Your center is not a means to getting something; money, a relationship, clothes. That is not why you're focusing in your center. If you are reading this for that, then you have missed the point of this book and you may feel desperate. Feeling desperate is a manifestation of another emotion and that is lack. Your center is the center of abundance which is just the opposite of feeling lack. You know you are aligned with your center when you are looking within you and around you and you feel grateful. You feel exhilarated and ready for the day. Even little moments of gratitude throughout your day can have a huge impact on your mood and energy. Gratitude makes it easier for life to open up wonderful things for you and bring you wonderful things.

Showing Gratitude in a Variety of Ways.

As I've stated a few times, your center is your place of love, joy, and peace, and when you are aligned with it, you want to show your gratitude. You want to express that to others.

One day, my landlord in my building came by to fix a bunch of stuff in my apartment. I was just too busy and I'll admit too lazy to do it myself. There was some painting that needed to be done, a ceiling fan that needed changing, some work done on the floor boards, simple things, but he was the best at doing it and so I let him do it. When he finished, I asked him was there anything I could buy him as a gift to show my appreciation.

"Red wine, Antonio. Red wine." He replied. I

was thinking, *Luis, you don't look like you need to be drinking.* He's an older man maybe between his late 50's to mid-60's, and I just didn't feel it would be good to get him that, but it was what he wanted so I planned to get it for him. Even though, I never did because I simply kept forgetting. Honestly, I felt gratitude for what he did, but really felt bad because every time I would see him in the building I would remember I hadn't gotten his red wine yet.

Fast forward a couple of months later, I called him to tell him about another issue in the apartment and he sounded sick. He'd been coming down with the flu. BOOM! I instantly felt this rush of excitement. Not because he was sick but because I had tons of medicine and natural herbs in my apartment I could give him. I literally ran down to his apartment and bombarded him with Vitamin B, Echinacea, Vitamin C, and blueberry extract. When I tell you, he was so happy, and so was I. It was the perfect way to really express my gratitude and he actually loved that more than me giving him the red wine. Point of the story is, when you give to someone you want it to fill your heart with joy and theirs too. If it doesn't do that, it probably won't be as beneficial. Even the good book (the Bible) says, "Give with a cheerful heart." That cheerful heart is your center. I always felt like the universe set that situation up to happen the way it did so I could learn that right there in that moment. It might seem small but it was a special and wonderful realization.

Getting Centered Exercise

1. **Meditate for three to five minutes every day:** You can use guided meditation or meditate without it. I have added a couple of recommendations in the appendix section in case you decide to use guided meditation. I recommend doing this first thing in the morning or right before you go to sleep. If you feel like you're doing it wrong or you can't focus, just keep doing it daily and trust that you'll improve.

2. **Create a list of fifteen things you're grateful for:** This may sound like a lot, but it's really not. Don't stop until you come up with fifteen things. This will challenge you to do some heavy thinking about what you're grateful for. Pull the list out at least once a day as a reminder that you have way more to be grateful for than to complain about.

3. **Call three people you haven't spoken to in a while and tell them how much you're**

grateful for them: Really think deeply about the people you're going to call before you speak with them. Conjure up the emotion of gratitude and then call them up with thoughts and feelings of gratitude. Oh, they'll feel amazing and loved, but the way it will make you feel will be priceless.

4. **Create a Gratitude Journal:** Begin writing in it once a day. Write down something you're grateful for every single day. Feel that gratitude within you. Don't stop writing until you do.

NOTES

CHAPTER 8

SIGNS AND WONDERS

This is How You Know it's Real

As the saying goes, the proof is in the pudding. It is my belief and my knowing that you can't believe the teachings of this book wholeheartedly without your life changing into something powerful, exhilarating and progressive. I don't want you to think that this is just some hocus pocus stuff because it isn't. But it takes your own personal experience to know! The reason I can write this book and write it with conviction is because I'm experiencing what it's like to be dominantly living within my center. In this chapter, we'll go through some ways to know when you are seeing life through your center and moments when you are not. This awareness will aid you in creating a life full of inspiration that will leave you satisfied.

When I was in college, I had a professor that whenever I would tell him about an issue, opportunity or challenge I was facing, he would give me this advice that at first I thought was really good advice. It's the good ole common sense advice we've heard from our friends, family members and even celebrities. *Hope for the best, but prepare for the worst.* This professor was someone I trusted and had always guided me with good advice when it came to school and balancing life. Well, this conventional wisdom felt right to me until well, until it didn't. Until I knew what I know now and then my energy and my knowledge of self could no longer accept that. Hope for the best, but prepare for the worst? *How in the hell did we as a society come to accept such low expectations?*

I always knew it was off just little bit. One day, after telling my professor I was looking forward to getting a high score on a test for another class, he proceeded to utter those dreadful words, "Well, Antonio, you know what I like to say, hope for the best and prepare for the worst." I decided it was the last time I would accept that saying.

I turned to him and said, "Unh, unh professor! Hope for the best and expect the best!"

His eyes nearly popped out of his head. The reaction on his face was priceless. He'd not heard it switched around like that before, but after explaining my rationale around it, he understood completely and actually agreed. Don't look forward to things probably going bad or not as you expect. Give all your attention, hope, desire, and belief to the fact that it can go exactly as you want it to be.

You Expect Good Things

When you thrive from your center more and more, you simply begin to expect good things to happen to you and to others. It becomes unconditional, not conditional. When you simply expect things to go well for you, you know your center is real! Your mind may try and bring you all kinds of thoughts of opposition to what you want, but you know deep down inside that you deserve the best, and you expect it. Expecting good things means you have aligned with your center, you believe it, and well, you accept it. Your dominant energy is that things are always working out for you and you don't just hope for it, you expect it.

You see, the reason people say hope for the best and prepare for the worst is because preparing for the worst serves as a precaution for safety or to avoid being disappointed and hurt. Many times, people expect the worst will happen more than they hope the best will. Their dominant belief is that they must leave room for the other shoes to drop and I'm here to tell you that you don't!

All of the abundance you want is there. All of the money you desire is there. All of the relationships and connections you desire are there. You just have to give your attention, knowledge and belief to that without doing the opposite at the same time.

Going to Meet the Queen

I will never forget the summer of 2007. I was seventeen years old and madly in love with Beyonce. I still am, but I've let Jay-Z take over for now. Beyonce had come to Miami to do a concert and I really wanted to go. Forget that, in my mind, I was going! I was literally telling everyone I knew, "You know I'm going to meet Beyonce, right?" For about a month, I was telling people I was going. No tickets, but somehow I knew I was going. Fast forward to the day of the show, I ironed my clothes, got all freshened up and even felt some butterflies in my stomach. I was tweaking, as we say in New York. About two hours before the show, the phone rang and my grandmother told me it was my cousin on the phone and she wanted to speak to me.

"Hey cousin, what's up?" I said.

"Nothing much, I wanted to see what you were up to." She responded. My heart was beating like an African drum. I could feel she was calling me about something major.

"I'm relaxing here with Grams." I said.

"Okay, okay. Cool. How fast do you think you can be ready?" She replied. I nearly jumped out of my body. I knew right then why she had asked me that. This was it! I was going to the show!

I dropped the phone, ran into the other room and threw on my clothes; damn near forgetting to put my shoes on in the process.

So what happened was, my aunt, who has done some work with Beyonce in the past, had an extra ticket to the show and had my cousin call to find out if I wanted to go. Beyonce actually used a sample from my aunt's first song she ever recorded called "Girls Can't Do What The Guys Do" for her song "Upgrade You." Anyways, it got even better, not only did I go, but I got to meet Beyonce.

Yes, I met her and hugged her, and told her how

much I loved her. It was a moment I will never forget.

It was years later when the universe reminded me of this happening and I realized it had a lot to do with my expectancy. When you allow yourself to hope for the best and expect the best despite what it looks like, you are aligned with your center and you will see incredible, powerful and brilliant results.

Others may wonder why or how, but you'll know the power of aligning with your center because you will have brought a manifestation as a direct result of being connected with it. Even when you don't see results right away, that expectancy begins to train you to expect the best and more of the best intentionally.

The First Manifestations

Check this out. Before I met Beyonce that night, I'd already met her! In my head that is, over and over and over again. What I mean by that is I could feel the realness of it. It was happening. I knew it before it happened. I knew it months before it happened! And no, I wasn't hallucinating. I believed what I saw was real. To be honest, had I not met her that night, I might have been a little disappointed, but it wouldn't have stopped me from believing it would happen because momentum was underway. *What do you mean by momentum, Antonio?* I'm glad you asked.

Momentum

The English Oxford Living Dictionary describes momentum as, the impetus and driving force gained by the development of a process or course of events.

What was the driving force behind me going to meet Beyonce that night? Or me moving to New York after knowing that I would since I was twelve years old? I'd thought about both situations so long, and believed them so much, without doubt, without fear, without worrying about the how, that it had to manifest! When you are aligned with your center more and more through meditation, prayer, good feelings, good thoughts, and good people, you begin to build momentum and marvelous things begin to actualize around you!

Having good momentum feels exhilarating. It feels like you have wings on your back and you're ready to fly. You don't feel anxious, you feel exhilarated. Really good momentum keeps more of the same coming into your life. Momentum is a great sign and it helps you feel that there is more on the way because there is. Maybe that's why I've met Beyonce a few times since that first time. I'll stop showing off now. You get the point though. The momentum of being at one with your center is that you are aligned with your center more and more and good things happen.

The same way you can have momentum going in the right direction, you can have it going in the wrong direction. Which is what that feeling of not being able to stop thinking negatively or feeling controlled by fear all the time feels like. To stop negative momentum, focus on something else where you have good momentum and do it long enough that the momentum of that good thing becomes the momentum of how you are feeling on all subjects, no matter what.

Clarity

Once you begin to feel momentum on a topic, the next thing you might notice is that you feel clear-minded. It's as if you know the next thing to do and the thing after that. You are no longer questioning yourself or asking everyone else what they think about your life. You know what to do and it's the best feeling ever. When you get clearly aligned with your center, all of your desires and how to accomplish them begin to come clearly into focus. Don't ask for it all to happen at once, it won't. Piece by piece, you notice that every decision you make toward the life you want feels right, and if it isn't, you still feel good because you learned something from it. Similar to meditation, sometimes clarity will come as a result of momentum, and sometimes momentum will come as a result of clarity. Both are powerful signs that you are aligned with your center and that you should keep going down the path you feel is right. No one can fill your path for you. No one can walk your path for you. Once you feel clarity and recognize it, it will empower you to keep going.

Manifestation of Desires

Although I have stated many times in this book that aligning with your center is not about gaining material things or making anything happen like you winning the lottery, being healed from sickness, losing weight or whatever your desire or dream may be, I have to push this point once again. It's critical to know. You don't align with your center to manifest things, but as a result of aligning with your center you manifest things. Did you catch that? This is one of the most powerful concepts that you have to understand if you plan to use this book to your advantage. Aligning with your center, thinking positively, feeling positively, all those things you should be doing simply to do, simply because it feels better to do . For so long we have learned how to put up with negative emotion and all the pain of it and it torments us. Many of us were never really taught that when you feel better, it's actually better for you. It's a truth. Align with your center because aligning with your center is who you really are, because aligning with your center feels good, because aligning with your center is good. And then the money, the relationships, the house, the friends, the success, all that will follow you. It's inevitable. Trust the process and be at peace simply for the good feeling of being at peace.

Getting Centered Exercise

1. What good things are you expecting and looking forward to happening in your life?

2. Write down 3 things you are looking forward to feeling clarity about. Why is it important to you to feel clarity on these particular topics?

3. Write down 3 emotions that you are going to set your intent to feel unconditionally and deliberately.

NOTES

CHAPTER 9

CENTER-UATIONS

Sometimes You Are, Sometimes You Aren't

Here it goes. I'm just going to say it. You will not feel aligned with your center on every single topic. BOOM! I know. I made you read this entire book just to tell you that. That's ok though, you can develop the ability of being connected with your center on all topics over time.

You offer a certain response to every single subject, person, and thing in your life. You have a relationship with every subject, person, place and thing in your life as well. The greatness of that relationship is based on many factors, but the main thing is your interaction with those people, places and things.

When it comes to dealing with work, you might feel like you're centered. You go to work each day excited! You feel exhilaration. You feel purposeful. You know what's going on within you concerning work and it's wonderful. On the other hand, when it comes to your spouse, you may not feel so centered. You may feel like I'm over this relationship. It's not going anywhere and I'm tired of trying and I don't know what to do. You also have a relationship with money. Yes. Money. You may go to work every single day and work hard for money but also talk about how money isn't that important to you.You don't have to be a lover of money but negative feelings about money can push it away from you. See what I mean? Guess what? That's okay! Let's get into how you can be centered in real life because all of the information in this book may sound incredible to you in theory, right? But how do you actually make sure you're being centered as much as possible in everyday life situations. Let's touch on a few subjects.

Your Center and Family

Having a bond with your family is extremely important. For many of us, the opinions and thoughts that our family have about us matter a whole lot. We look for our family to back us up on important decisions. We look for them to support our businesses, events and even parties. The importance of family cannot be stressed enough. Family is necessary. Yet, what happens when you do things that your family doesn't agree with? What happens when you bring a guy home that dad isn't too fond of? Or when you decide to move across the country or world to pursue your dreams and family is telling you that you're making a mistake.

Being connected with your center means knowing and following your deepest truths even when family doesn't agree with you. It means to be able to stand firm in any decision you make no matter who agrees or not, because you know that it's a decision based on what's true for you. This is not easy and some people never develop the courage to stand up for themselves when it comes to family.

Remember in chapter one, we talked about being conditioned and programmed at birth? It goes right back to that. I had a friend of mine growing up that was extremely attached to her mom and her mom was attached to her. Actually, attached might be an understatement. They did everything together. She and I were the same age. We both went to the same church, and our moms are really good friends. I remember when we were seniors in high school and I was talking about going away for college and I was telling her mother my plans, she immediately screamed out, "No! I will not let Nicki go away for college. It's too much craziness out there in the world." In my mind, I was thinking "wow! You literally just made one of the biggest decisions for her that she should be making for herself." Now, don't get me wrong, I understood that out of love every parent wants what's best for their child.

Any mother would, but at eighteen and embarking on a new journey, I also felt that it should have been Nicki's decision not her mom's. Of course, out of respect for her mom, instead of going away for college, Nicki enrolled in the local community college and stayed at home under the guidance and watchful eye of her mother. What was disappointing for me was knowing that she wanted to go away for school but didn't want to go against the authority of her mother. Now, I'm not saying she didn't do well in life and succeed by staying home and going to a local college. You can succeed anywhere if you believe, work smart, and do what you have to; but to know she sacrificed her true happiness long-term for her mother's did not really allow her to spread her wings.

I recently talked to this same friend, and years later she tells me one of her biggest regrets was not going away for college.

Being aligned with your center takes courage. It takes tenacity and it takes a willingness to put that voice inside of you first. Strong family bonds matter and family is truly one of the most important parts of life, but sometimes your calling and your direction will not be what your family believes in, likes, or even agrees with. You've got to trust your guidance, your intuition, your knowing, that you're following the path that works for you and the outcome of your choices will prove it later on. And if it all falls down and you fail by following your deepest intuition, that's fine too. Every disappointment and failure just helps you clarify and be better for the next time. Knowing you followed your center and what is true for you, even when it's uncomfortable, is one of the best feelings you can have.

Your Center and Work

Work. This is a big one. I say that because many people simply hate their job! Absolutely hate it. They hate where they work, how long they work, who they work with and even the route to work. Some people literally spend every day thinking about the end of the day just because they hate their job and don't like their work. Welp! I'll be the first to say, that used to be me! It was literally the hardest thing to do, going to work in the morning. If you're living your life like that then you're not living, you're existing. Work is where many of us spend ninety percent of our time, and if you can't at least like it, you're not truly receiving all the benefits of work.

Work is supposed to inspire you and you inspire your work. The only way to feel like that at work is to be aligned with your center. When you're aligned with your center and you're working, you're so focused, energized and creative, the day just flies by. Well, usually, there are exceptions. But mostly, you feel those feelings and it's exhilarating.

Feel Your Purpose

So what's the key? PURPOSE! When you feel a sense of purpose, it changes your outlook on work forever. I don't care if you're a janitor, a banker, or an engineer. When you feel purposeful, you bring your work to life. When you are one with your center, your purpose becomes clearer every day. Your biggest purpose in any situation is to simply be you. When you are aligned with your center, you bring your entire personality, charm, wit, skill, love, and intelligence to the table and it shows.

Boss and Co-workers

One of the biggest pains at work can be your boss and your co-workers. I know this from firsthand experience. You won't necessarily like everyone that works with you and they won't necessarily like you either, but it's all about how you let it affect you. It also matters how much of it consumes your focus. When you are aligned with your center, those people, sometimes, slowly but surely, either change how they react to you, move around you or for some reason just don't affect you the same way. Why is that? Because to be connected and aligned with your center is to feel love, to feel gratitude, to feel purposeful. If you're around anyone at work that isn't exuding that and you are, they won't be able to take it for very long or they'll change!

Not a Quick Fix

If you make it a habit to meditate before work or clear your mind before work or make a list of all the things you're grateful for before work, it's going to be a lot easier to deal with people in a variety of situations. You'll be more focused on your purpose and what you want to accomplish while at work versus what everyone else is thinking about you and that might not have anything to do with you.

Your Center and Relationships

When I say relationships, I'm also including friendships. Relationships play a huge part in shaping our character, our desires, beliefs and our wants. Who we choose to have a relationship with reflects to the world what we accept and how much we truly love ourselves. When you live your life from a place of being aligned with your center, you attract a partner that also lives the majority of their life from their center. When you two come together, it's nothing short of magic. There is no pressure to outdo each other or jealousy or envy, just love. If there is competition, it's healthy competition from a place of inspiration to help each other be better. When you're with this person, it feels wonderful, but when you're not, you still feel complete because you're not loving them from a place of attachment but from a place of connectedness. You're connected to the love within you and it radiates to your partner and vice versa. This is really what everyone wants. It's only when you get with someone because you're lonely, or hurt and you begin demanding that they be everything in the world for you that you soon find yourself disappointed. No one can be everything to you. A person can only be who they are.

Control Self

No matter what, you can never control the actions of another person. You can only control your reactions and responses to another person. Being aligned with your center in a relationship is true freedom. You don't feel bogged down or stuck or controlled. You feel free. You feel worthy. When you are in this state, you actually have more to give to your partner because you're also sharing that feeling of freedom with them. No matter how much you love someone and they love you, everyone needs to feel a sense of freedom within self.

Getting Centered Exercise

No matter what you do or where you are, you have to deal with people:

Family, bosses, co-workers, strangers, friends, boyfriends and girlfriends. To get the most out of these relationships, you need to bring all of you, your whole self, fully connected and aligned with your center, healed and clear-minded to the table. When you do this, it literally transforms your life.

1. **Focus on how you feel about people, not so much about how they feel about you:** When you do this, you'll notice that you have control over what goes on in your mind and how you are going to view each and every situation.

2. **Remember others actions are a reflection of what's going on within them, how they were raised, what they believe, and their mood about life in that moment.**

3. **Visualize yourself being a great communicator when you aren't with people:** Picture how you want your relationships to flow, and eventually, it will come to fruition just the way you desire.

4. **Write a letter to a family member, a friend, or your partner about the way you want your relationship with them to be:** You can keep this letter private if you choose to. By writing it out, you're helping yourself align even more with the essence of how you want those relationships to be.

NOTES

CHAPTER 10

DEEPEST REALIZATIONS/IT'S ALL GOOD

When I got the idea to write this book, I really couldn't believe I was thinking about writing a book. There I was twenty-six years old and getting the idea to write a book. No doubt I've gotten a lot of ideas in my life, but it has been my choice, like yours as well, whether to act on those ideas or let them die within me. It took me over two years to bring my book to life. After I decided to write this book, nothing else mattered.

Knowing Your Power

We are all presented with the power of choice every single day. Every single day, you have an opportunity to align with your center. You get to pick what you'll do. We choose what we eat, what we wear, who we love, how we respond to life, and most importantly, how we spend our time. Having choices is true freedom. Making a choice is your power! It starts from within. It starts from knowing that the power of choice is available to you at all levels at all times no matter what. No one can take away your ability to make a choice about everything that concerns you, especially from within. When you're looking at life from your center, you find that you make more of the right choices.

5 Steps Forward 3 Steps Back

Mistakes help you focus within your center. I can't tell you how many times I thought that I had figured out how to get past a certain issue only to find myself right back dealing with the same issue again and again. Learning from your mistakes is important, and surely, you want to avoid making the same mistakes over and over again, but the fact is, some mistakes you will repeat over and over again. Once you truly decide that you're going to move on from making those mistakes and learn from those mistakes, you will then go on to make new ones and it's okay! Mistakes are just opportunities to evaluate your progress, growth, and willpower. The last thing you want to do is beat yourself up over your mistakes. Instead, do your best to focus within your center and gain awareness on what's holding you back. Use mistakes and failure as teaching moments. Critique yourself without criticizing yourself. It could be something as small as changing your perspective, changing the set of friends you hang out with and/or building new habits; rather thought habits, feeling habits, or both. See mistakes as pit stops helping you get to your destination.

Be Unmoved

Life never stops presenting us with challenges and problems. Life also offers us many solutions to our problems as well. We find solutions to our problems when we focus within in our center. Therefore, make a decision that you will not be disturbed by the ups and downs of life. Change your mental attitude to that of knowing that in the end, all will be well. Look ahead and beyond the troubles of today. Bask in knowing that your life can and will improve in the long run. There is no obstacle to a great life other than your own thinking about it.

The Final Thought

I realized something a couple of years ago; I've mastered the art of bouncing back! No matter what problems, issues, failures, and disappointments I encounter. I've mastered the art of bouncing back! The greatest thing to remember is that your center is within you and that no matter how separated or down you may feel at times, you can always realign with it because it is the center of who you really are! I can remember a few times I've thought, *Whoa. This is a lot. I don't know how I'm going to get over this hump.* I always do and I always come through the fire stronger and better. And so do you! It's in you. You will figure it out. You will realize the next step. Don't give up or give in to doubt, worry and fear. Don't fret over the small stuff because it's all small stuff; even the big stuff is small stuff because your purpose in life is greater than any challenge you could ever face. You have comeback power, my friend! Begin to align with your center daily and watch every aspect of your life begin to change. I'm excited for you! Take these words from this book with you. Realize you've got comeback power. The answers to all of your problems are within you. Get ready. If you choose to apply what you've read deliberately and intentionally, your life could change forever. You've been through enough pain. It's time for the next level. Have the faith that your life is becoming something amazing. Why not you? It's time to live your best centered life now!

Getting Centered Exercise

1. **Write down three tools from this book you could utilize for the rest of your life:** How will you make it a habit to use these tools?

2. **Share this book with someone else you know that could benefit from it:** What's one thing you'll share with them that made thing book helpful for you.

3. **Right down three choices you are going to make right now that will help you align with your center on purpose each day.**

NOTES

THE CENTER IN REVIEW.

CHAPTER BY CHAPTER.

1. **You didn't simply become the person you are today on your own.** Many of the things that make up your mindset, your essence, and your very being, were programed into you and were done without your permission. In the first chapter, we explored what being programmed and conditioned does to us when that programming is negative and not positive. You can change the program.

2. **I called this chapter The Core because everything that we believe in is really the basis for what's happening in our lives:** Your core beliefs shape your world; they represent who you are and how you see the world. The programs we were taught created beliefs in us. Our beliefs are what keep certain things flowing to us and away from us. Remember to

examine your beliefs about everything. Your core is powerful.

3. **If we could only get rid of all of our negative thinking, we'd be fine, right?** Well, you can't get rid of it completely, but you can change how it affects you, and that's more than enough! We focused on how to think about what you want effectively and how to do less of thinking the opposite. This tool is vital to being centered more often than not.

4. **Chapter 4 explored what this book is about in the first place:** Being connected to your center. In this chapter, we focused on how our habits around what we feel holds the power to our growth. Your feeling habits and thought habits are a part of you.

5. **After I wrote about beliefs, thoughts, and feelings, we got into Dreaming Again.** Dreaming Again is about using the power of your mind to see what others may not see in your future and understanding the power of doing that intentionally.

6. **Dreaming again is not enough:** You don't want to be one of those people sitting around dreaming and hoping you bring your dreams into reality, right? Right! Remember to visualize the wonderful possibilities of your life. Look forward to your vision manifesting and never seize doing that.

7. **In this chapter, we talked about where your true power is:** After this chapter, I hope you felt like a boss. Like someone that is centered and ready to use the tools in this chapter to align with your center and bring your best life forward!

8. **Follow the signs because they are everywhere:** Oh yes, they are. Here, we discussed what it means to have some momentum going in your life and experiencing clarity like never before. It's signs and wonders that show you that you're moving in the right direction. Always look for the signs.

9. **Look, the tools in this book mean nothing if you can't use them in relationships, friendship and real-life center-uations:** Yes, center-uations! And I called it that because

when you align with your center, all relationships are different and feel different. You also learned how we tend to be center-focused around certain issues more than others. It's a fact. But it's all good, we're all working to be more centered, and that's what this book is about. Refer back to this chapter often when building relationships with others.

10. **We all have opportunities to make powerful choices:** When you are conscious of this daily, it's life-changing. This chapter closes the book and leaves you reflecting on more.

FROM THE AUTHOR

Thank you for reading *The Center: How Our Thoughts, Feelings, and Beliefs Shape Our Destiny.*

If you'd like notifications on new releases and upcoming projects, join my email list at AntonioJavar.com/inspiredliving.

Thank you!

-Antonio J. Hairston

ACKNOWLEDGMENTS

To my best friends: Nydia Fonseca, Terell Depina, Jaron Keith, Eric Garcia, Krystal Rodriguez, Frank Sepulveda, Deeon Brown, Mike Rickman, Dubem Okeke, Tommy Hawkins, your friendships have been essential to my soul and I love each and every one of you and you are appreciated. Valentina Alexandria for your motivation to move with urgency and get this book done. You are incredible queen. Darius Thomas, thank you for styling me. You are superior and skilled at what you do. Kiwanis White, my FAMUly. Thank you for all the helpful advice. Geo Derice for doing my cover. You and your team are incredible. Thank you for sharing your knowledge and wisdom with me throughout this process. You are a trooper and a real one. Last but not least, to God for guiding me and giving me the wisdom to see this book through to the finish line. The Center. It is done.

56683251R00077

Made in the USA
Middletown, DE
23 July 2019